Little Childr

THE TOWER
OF BABEL

Retold by Anne de Graaf   Illustrated by José Pérez Montero

BROADMAN
& HOLMAN
PUBLISHERS

THE TOWER OF BABEL

Published in 1998 by Broadman & Holman Publishers,
Nashville, Tennessee

Text copyright © 1998 Anne de Graaf
Illustration copyright © 1998 José Pérez Montero
Design by Ben Alex
Conceived, designed and produced by Scandinavia Publishing House

Printed in Singapore
ISBN 0-8054-1783-4

Where do you live? What country?
Do you know how to say "hi!" in
any other languages? Mhoro!

Czesc! Hola! That's the Shona language of Zimbabwe, Poland and Mexico!

A long, long, long time ago, everyone spoke only one language.

We speak the same language. Say "hi!" Say it louder! I hear you and say "hi!" back.

A long, long, long time ago, as people spread out to live, they still understood each other.

Hey you! Pick up that grain of sand! No, not that one, THAT one! He knows what I mean.

10

11

Then some people found a flat place
and decided to make it their home.

I like flat places, it makes it easy to build on. The next time you play in the sand, clear a flat place before you build your tower.

The people said, "Let's make bricks and bake them until they're very hard."

The people were clever. Instead of using stones they made these bricks, and stuck the bricks together with tar, instead of mortar.

Build a tower with your fists, one on top of the other, on top of the other, on top of the other. . . . Where will it stop?

17

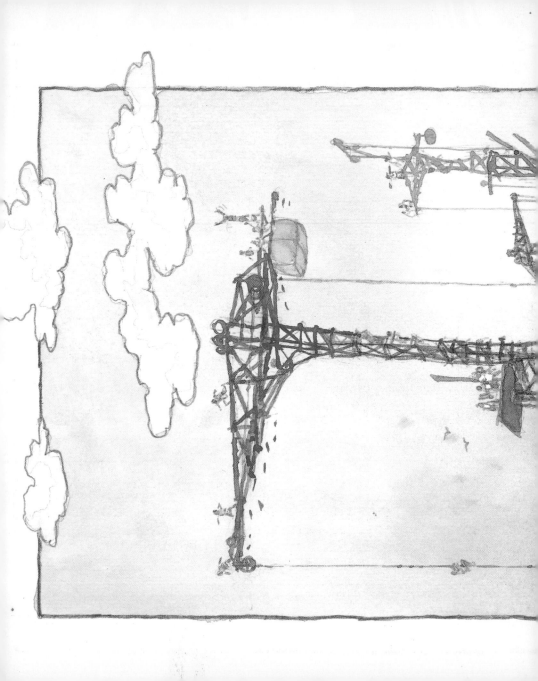

They thought they were a very, very, very, very smart, smarter, WAY TOO SMART, all-the-way-to-the-heavens people.

They wanted to build a very, very, very, very good, better, *WAY TOO GOOD*, all-the-way-to-the-heavens city.

These people said, "We can be
famous and not have to wander
anymore."

Then the people said, "Come, let's build ourselves a city! We will finally have a home."

Now a tower wasn't good enough. They had great plans!

29

When God saw what the people were trying to do, He knew He must stop them, or they would think they were gods.

They were a very, very, very, very proud, prouder, WAY TOO PROUD, all-the-way-to-the-heavens people.

So God mixed up their words and made different languages. The people no longer spoke one language, but many.

Heavens! If workers don't understand each other, I could say, "Get that grain of sand!" and he would think I meant, "Hand me the hammer!" That's no way to build something.

33

The city they never finished building was called Babel, which means *Mixed Up and Confused*, because there the Lord mixed up the language of the whole world.

Sometimes small is better, even if all you end up with is an anthill . . . as long as you're not too proud of it.

35

Then the Lord sent all the people wandering, spreading them out all over the earth.

Adiós!
Czesc!
Chisarai zvakanaka!

A NOTE TO THE Big PEOPLE:

The *Little Children's Bible Books* may be your child's first introduction to the Bible, God's Word. In *The Tower of Babel*, detailed illustrations make the eleventh chapter of Genesis spring to life. This is a DO book. Point things out, ask your child to find, seek, say, and discover.

Before you read these stories, pray that your child's little heart would be touched by the love of God. These stories are about planting seeds, having vision, learning right from wrong, and choosing to believe.

A little something fun is said in italics by the narrating animal, to make the story come alive. In this DO book, wave, wink, hop, moo, or do any of the other things the stories suggest so this can become a fun time of growing closer. Pray together after you read this. There's no better way for big people to learn from little people.